Black Lotus

Table Of Contents

Forest Bathing

Toxic Masculinity

Bloodletting

toxic masculinity perpetuated by a broken society
unrealistic socially reinforced prejudice
anger,

betrayal by those thought forever loyal
class warfare's mentally imposed shackles
frustration,

slithering tongues damage to self confidence
tainted memories of violent altercations
paranoia,

acceptance of coping through alcoholism
looming threat of student loan fueled indentured servitude
anxiety,

bloodlet
or bleed to death

Pieces

grey and numb
remnants hang on the outside of me,
grey and numb
threads dangle from the hole in my chest,
grey and numb
each shape bursts forth from a ravine of iniquity,

a memory triggers
the colors flood
a response meant for a past aggressor
distributed unjustly
the innocent leave
the memory fades,

grey and numb
my pieces chime in the winter winds

Another Day

heart flying
sweat pouring
real or fiction
past or present
why is it all merging?

unable to sleep
the smallest creak
knife in hand
attack the sound
your demons have come to claim you

feel a presence
a shift in the room
eyes open
grab the gun
before dread consumes you

no one is here
but you'd better check
adrenaline rush
listen close
maybe they can hear you

6 a.m.
senses dull
ready to quit
sun is up
time to work

It's Fine

event after event
always something to blame
overlooking the truth
deep below the surface

cover the cracks
fill the pavement with alcohol
war stories
always strength, never damage

black it out
emotion isn't needed
love is gone
success will fix you

quick health check
below the surface
no surprise
the faults have grown

a little deeper
it should be okay

how odd

the foundation is crumbling

Helpless

blood-soaked stripped shirt
the video still burns in my head
moans of agony
intubated on an S.I.C.U bed

should have been sitting next to him
foot surgery rearranged fate's thread
tripped on the body next to him
couldn't escape, so he played dead

oxycodone haze
on the waiting room floor
poster boards of hope we create
the days become a blur

mistaken for opening day theatrics
the tear gas grenades pop
screams ring out
the bodies, start to drop

pain in his words
describing methodical killing
heart hurts
passive courtroom listening

outside we praise his resilience

he shouldn't have to do this alone

we are taught strength is silence

unfortunately, we are men

What Lurks Beneath

The Grey

the soldier who mans the gate grey
has perfected the state of numb

> it happens now, randomly
> tears spill from windows

emotional dissonance for survival
it's best to ignore the weight's sum

> confusing, the irrationality
> why the sudden flood?

hypervigilance to protect the owner
he can't know the door is broken

> back to groggy and grey
> over as quick as it began

water breaches the top, occasionally
but the floodgates, they mustn't open

> the feelings, they never stay
> but something, something is wrong

Non-Member

white kid growing in a black neighborhood
tries hard but doesn't fit in

across town for sports with other white kids
tries hard but doesn't fit in

links up with the smart kids
tries hard but doesn't fit in

attempts to just be himself
picked on

attempts to dress like the kids at school
picked on

attempts to act like his peers
picked on

hangs out with gang members
accepted, but doesn't fit in

hangs out on the block
understood, but doesn't fit in

argues with parents for understanding
no common ground, can't fit in

tries to work in America professionally
speech to ideology, can't fit in

finds peace in another country
obviously, impossible to fit in

it's believed humans are inherently social
I'm not one, I can't fit in

Loyalty (poem by Dee Rose)

I've bled for it
mental pain manifested into the physical
it's because my dedication is deeply rooted
and then ripped out like a weed in summer
trampled in the dirt by an aggressive runner
then leaving a bloody mess in its wake

I've cried over it
there's nothing worse than when the feeling's not mutual
tears of abandonment when it maneuvers to neutral
sprinting away from me with great speed
even though, I'm its greatest champion
it makes me feel as though I'm not worthy

I've worshipped it
praised others for giving it its due
because I know it's the only thing besides love that's true
when it's reciprocated, it's the ultimate joy
it empowers all whom it embraces
it produces smiles even though it remains faceless

I live it
I breathe it
I love it
I heed it
I want it
I need it

Run!

ignored with chain distractions
the unrelenting march of stress
thoughts of inadequacy stuck on replay
capitalisms molding of unnecessary necessities
driving the suffocation of self-worth
social media propagating fabricated lifestyles
rhythm lost amidst, these artificial lives
out of sync, lost in an ocean of the lost

under this false composure
if only things would click,
I would flee society's enclosure
the cage door would get a swift kick
reject the negativity saturating my bones
breathe without dream crushing indoctrinated expectations
break the binding shackles of student loans
explore without constricting financial limitations

but things do not click
for people like me

my resources are thin
my life is survival

I will die here
just like the rest

This year

the year you long for the presence of another human
the worldwide pandemics smothering isolation
burn a little for fuel then over the shoulder

the year you return to the cell you struggled to escape
an auto-immune disease taking shape
burn a little for fuel then over the shoulder

the year you carry a pistol on every out of the house trip
a looming threat from a trey deuce Crip
burn a little for fuel then over the shoulder

the year you can't seem to scrub enough blood out of your car
rushing your brother from a drunken accident to the ER
burn a little for fuel then over the shoulder

the year your paranoia has you preparing for war
confronting a gang OG to settle a score
burn a little for fuel then over the shoulder

the year your brother is shot at a movie premier
another mass shooting endemic to America's atmosphere
burn a little for fuel then over the shoulder

the year you lose the family you think you created
self-destruction after a promiscuous girl you dated
burn a little for fuel then over the shoulder

the year you get jumped for the ideology you uphold
punching an OG who is trying to assault a 16-year-old
burn a little for fuel then over the shoulder

the year your friend calls in agony uncontrolled
his sister shot dead at 17 years old
burn a little for fuel then over the shoulder

the year you pass the crime scene in between blocks
a friend's mother murdered in front of the mailbox
burn a little for fuel then over the shoulder

the year your first love slits her wrists
psychological torture simply because she exists
burn a little for fuel then over the shoulder,

the year you finally understand what you always knew
this year is every year the trauma remains whole
and this year is the year it finally stops you
a brain overflowing with unprocessed emotional coal

Her ring

warmth from a past long gone
leaps to life as it comes into view
insides no longer numb
happiness manages to break through

hesitation to leave my seat
must push through the fear
it's okay to feel love, a little
even if she isn't here,

a short walk in perfect weather
breathing in the nostalgic view
a historic mansion of white and red
the sky for once, a clear blue

happy anticipation as the hinges creek
old leather couches and the antique car
smile as my shoes tap the hardwood floor
glance into the whiskey bar

contentment fills my chest
a renewed urge to explore
to the carpeted stairwell
and up to the second floor

a wooden plank creaks
the memories of her flood
my eyes fill with water
my hands coat with blood

a private midnight tour
by an employee most kind
we were so outrageously lucky
how could I have been so blind

not being able to live without another
matters not when you push them away
poisoned to the core, or so I thought
murdered our relationship with my decay

we took a picture here
on this stairwell in front of this mirror
you and I were happy once
the picture couldn't have been clearer

ended things between us
sealed my pain in a pastel coffin
hid it in the depths of my mind
separate from the me that is rotten

purposely ignored the action's weight
but soon realized it was an impossibility
had to try to win you back
to show how much you meant to me

pictures and construction paper
a two-room grandstand play
a cheesy self-made storybook
and chocolates on display

at the end of the book, a ring
but the damage had already been done
it was too late
the rot, my poison, had already won

it was never meant to resurface
but it will not stay buried
the coffin just keeps screaming
it was you I should have married

Forest Bathing

Where did it go?

anger on the onion peeled back
an ocean of sadness underneath
volatile weather encroaching newly found peace
tenacity now weathering the attack

illness, mental and physical
subdued previously by sheer wrath
freely distorting the traveled path
digging this deep doesn't feel natural

sifting through the sorrow
two layers in, looking for an out
hoping a single bud will sprout
how deep did happiness burrow?

The Black Lotus

in murky lake water floating
her silent mystique stilled my heart,
poisoned from my past, slowly decaying
I was trying not to fall apart,
her beauty distracted from the pain inside
her intellect refreshing, and for a time I forgot,

the warmth of sunlight hitting skin
kindness which I had never known,

the calm of nature's most serene sight
support in which the world could be grown,

fresh mountain air, her smile
interaction with her body of any kind,

water on a sweltering summer day
conversation quenching the thirst of a mind,

too busy ignoring my own inner peril
her murky water, I didn't even acknowledge,
still, she planted and nurtured a seed
deep below my rot, without my knowledge,

while my past continued to fester
she became my world
25 years of poison I started to remember
my thinking flipped
numb and black, I saw myself,
for her I could not empathize
bankrupt, my inner wealth,
I had nothing left to give

dead inside, a reoccurring thought
logical thinking I tried,
let her go, she deserves better
it was painful to decide,

I placed her back into the lake
not knowing what I had done,
the wounds she healed, I would not know
for many years to come,

the seed she planted is now blooming
but the lotus herself, is long gone
somewhere out there, still floating

--To Candice Konishi,
Wherever you float in life,
I hope you find the happiness you deserve. --

Growth

amidst everything black and dead
hope itself has joined the rubble

scoured to core for warmth that fled
finding only ruminations trouble

only with fight's dying breath
does it make itself known

birthed through decay and death
in rotten soil it has grown

the only piece that hasn't died
a single green leaf where there are none

happy thoughts cast aside
the real work has just begun

Therapy

tic toc EMDR clicks through memories past
the dark corridors seal is broken,
box after box reveal the pain by processing
find out why will has finally broken,

crushing weight, restricting breath, fear floods
pitch black, senses scream, death is approaching,

stop the bleeding and offer support
each time a younger you was broken,
room by room parts left to fend for themselves
step inside and feel again each time a heart was broken,

muscles surge, kill the threat, anger as defense
can't fight, too late, death is approaching,

talk about the truth of your reality
normal human responses before you were broken,
address what has happened and foster new growth
the only way to repair what has been broken

金継ぎ (Kintsugi)

puzzle of a brain shattered on the floor
a heart's pieces snipped from the hole
self-reflection as empty eyes meet the mirrors glaze
over thirty years but finally fully razed

tears, dreams, ambition,
water, gold, lacquer,
mix

piece by piece my mentality will be reset
piece by piece my heart will become golden

~~~~~~

A single piece of you can grow
into something extraordinary.

No matter how downtrodden or broken you are,
find that piece.

Nurture it.

With time it will bloom like the mythical black lotus.

~~~~~~

COMING SOON

NINETEEN
BECOMING WHOLE

www.erinjaymoyer.com

ABOUT THE AUTHOR

Erin Jay Moyer is a poet, novelist, and a lover of language with a degree in linguistics. After releasing Black Lotus he intends to finish the second novel in his dystopian action adventure series, 'NINETEEN'. Past poetry books have included: 'Even A Rose Has Thorns' and 'The Unknown Poet: introduction to society'. Erin has traveled through Guatemala and Honduras to record speakers of the Ch'orti' language. He spent two years living in Japan and teaching English. He has recently returned to America to pursue a career as a writer and a computational linguist.

Books By This Author

Nineteen: A Hero's Rise

Our nation's wealth disparity finally caught up. The fight against the wealthiest one percent ripped America apart. Recreational drugs created and weaponized by the government have turned citizens into addicts. The remaining police have formed gangs to assert control. The one percent have relocated to cities that are sectioned off by giant walls.

Amid the chaos, Kai preaches that there is more to living than just surviving. He encourages his group of waste landers to find things worth living for. Before anyone in his group is able to come to such a revelation, Kai is murdered. Nineteen reluctantly steps in as the interim leader and the group sets their sights on revenge.

Along the road to payback they find themselves on the front lines of a war they thought had long ended. Joining forces with unlikely allies, they take on their oppressors in attempt to attain lives worth living.

Even A Rose Has Thorns

In this poetic novel an adolescent is struggling to figure out who he is and to find his place amongst the rest of the world. When his mother is diagnosed with a neuro muscular disease he rebels against societies accepted path and begins creating a path of his own. While opening his eyes to the world his path is riddled with murder, incarcerations, lost love, and the realities of poverty. Every poem plays a role in creating the bigger picture as the young man comes full circle along his path. Will he reach the person he has been trying to become or will his thorns get the best of him?

Introduction To Society

Enter this world through a poets perspective as you witness the trials and tribulations of Erin Jay Moyer. Become a part of his journey starting today.